(Lo, how the wars of the past have duly inured to you,
and the wars of the present also inure)
Then turn, and be not alarm'd O Libertad—turn your undying face,
To where the future, greater than all the past,
Is swiftly, surely preparing for you.

—WALT WHITMAN

note to the reader

This book takes as its focus the U.S. engagement in Iraq, and as its protagonist a modern-day Aeneas. A meditation on the god of war that has driven the national self into the region, it takes on various incarnations and voices of that god of war. The work is propelled by some questions: Who is this goddess of war in me? Where do I find the war in myself? How is the self connected to the national self, the one who makes war? Am I making war? What is the national self searching for? Where does "the enemy" exist in me? Is the enemy a guest, and is a guest an enemy? Who is the beloved? After the first few poems, the book traces the course of the war, so that there is a kind of overarching narrative for the reader to follow.

and **Aeneas stares** into her **helmet**

Tiffany Higgins

Poetry Series #11

CAROLINA WREN PRESS
Durham, North Carolina

Editor: Patrick Herron
Series Editor: Andrea Selch

Design: Lesley Landis Designs
Cover Image: "Western" © 2008 Pablo Ortega López
Author Photograph: Andrea Ferreira

*The mission of Carolina Wren Press is to seek out, nurture and promote literary
work by new and underrepresented writers, including women and writers of color.*

Carolina Wren Press is a 501(c)3 non-profit organization supported in part by
grants and generous individual donors. In addition, we gratefully acknowledge the
ongoing support of Carolina Wren Press's activities made possible through gifts to
the Durham Arts Council's United Arts Fund.

Library of Congress Cataloguing-in-Publication Data:

Higgins, Tiffany, 1970-
And Aeneas stares into her helmet / by Tiffany Higgins.
    p. cm. -- (Poetry series ; #11)
ISBN 978-0-932112-57-6
I. Title. II. Series.

PS3608.I367A84 2009
811'.6--dc22

2008050517

contents

in the year of my birth I am waiting to become

    in the year of my birth I am waiting to become / 1

disconcerted I hear still a calling

    I am in my bunker, waiting / 5

I wanted that death and so

    my major and I / 9

    I wanted that death and so / 14

and Aeneas comes upon the flaming city

    and Aeneas comes upon the flaming city / 17

    and the walls impregnable of centuries are falling / 18

    Aeneas in the oval office / 19

    Aeneas & the pilgrim child set out into the city / 21

    I think I do not know that Europe / 22

    over drifts of sand come I / 23

and a one-ton bomb named Moab tilts over Baghdad

    in these months we wait for eruptions / 27

    they say the war has begun over there / 28

    these are the days of nothing but triumph / 29

    I am a little pilgrim child / 30

here inside as of old the sandbox

    Aeneas in the airport / 33

    I am at my stance in Basra / 34

    here inside as of old the sandbox / 35

    america I think may be a kind of codeword / 36

    where is the war? / 37

    the war it writes me a letter / 38

freedom is walking itself on a leash

  and I am myself war / 41

  a sheaf of war / 42

  freedom is walking itself on a leash / 43

the visitor pays a visit to the Statue of Liberty

  the visitor pays a visit to the Statue of Liberty / 47

when I get to the bottom of the city I cry out

  ample upon the painted sands / 51

  when I get to the bottom of the city I cry out / 52

  I lead my people into a dome gold-foiled / 53

  I take myself a tour of Nineveh / 54

Interrogation #2356

  Interrogation #2356 / 57

you, there, back behind beginning

  in the end you implode me / 61

  I have met the enemy, and— / 62

  I search in you my own destruction / 64

  when smoke arises from the tube car nostrils / 65

  I wake up to become my own terrorist / 66

  I walk slowly into the field where I await myself / 67

  bellum omnium contra omnes / 68

  I hope you don't mind if I wiretap you / 69

crossing New York Harbor by ferry

  crossing New York Harbor by ferry / 73

finally I am the star of my own beheading video

  why didn't the flowers? / 81

  discourse on impossibility / 82

  finally I am the star of my own beheading video / 83

  and Aeneas appears on the reality show / 85

Aeneas in the Baghdad market

    I wake up in the middle of the night / 89

    it is my war / 93

    Aeneas on the public road / 94

    and Aeneas stares into her helmet (I) / 95

    school shooting / 100

    Aeneas at the Baghdad market / 101

in the beginning: lines from an ancient Babylonian tablet

    they have come too soon / 105

    lines from an ancient Babylonian tablet / 107

    birds of Iraq / 112

and Aeneas stares into her helmet

    and Aeneas stares into her helmet (II) / 115

deleted scene: **Aeneas in Carthage**

    Aeneas in Carthage / 121

notes / 132

acknowledgements / 133

in the year of my birth I am waiting to become

in the year of my birth I am waiting to become

in the year of my birth I am waiting to become

> meanwhile many sharpshooters train their sights
> on targets distant and not so distant

wavering   equivocal   I wander
half in, half out of existence

> and the form unintent on being me shilly-shallies, considers many possibilities
> to manifest even as an asteroid, eyelid-fluttering

or perhaps as disinclination itself, which as you must know
has set up its chain stores throughout the galaxy

> there am I   and am not
> thick with indecision

when to my lair in non-being wafts
a steady napalm of morning

> it excites my nostrils and sets me heaving
> toward a world on the other side of the not-yet-being

of that more solid world it must be said I bear too little knowledge
(even a life of microbes and assassinations has scarce set off this assessment)

> thick with unknowing—and so I arrive
> touching down before the doorstep of a two-story Colonial

in a suburb outside the marsh, filled in, of a firm Boston
beckoning the white-framed address from the front of a beautiful palisade

> garage door opener and closer securely in place
> and from the screened-in porch the television skitters its black and white buzz

> *In Ohio, students on a hill at a state…*

1

like Jack and Jill they went up a hill to fetch a pail of—
and Jack fell down and broke his crown and they both came tumbling—

    and there was no horror but the silence of the lawn
    as rope-green villages were falling

      it was war that brought me in you know
      nothing else could have lured me

disconcerted I hear still a calling

I am in my bunker, waiting

behind the house (white, green-shuttered) the rise, leafen, of a hill
a small wood (and within the small wood, a great rock)

    I go out in the back yard where I have hidden the dead
    I have preserved them perfectly well

behind the white house the great oaks
amidst the great oaks, the maples

    below the maples, the big rock we climb on to see from
    and below the big rock, centuries of drifting leaves

no one rakes them up they just sift and wait
one year don't know why I get the urge to gather up

    my money cool green bills
    and lay it below the leaves

I choose a corner of the great rock as a landmark
(I did not hear winter or even think of it)

    the green bills I had saved
    buried deep in soil

(autumn came and then the snow)
and the branches blacken drift their tears of white

    leaking down onto the leaves, the leaves
    finally when the crocuses have begun their song

I tromp out to the great rock
and dig where I remember

    I put my bank account
    hands squinching down through layers

wet wet wonder
in search of the cool green dry of paper

      oh, but where can it be, the money!
      didn't I just leave it right here, for remembrance!

he must have taken it, my brother
(and I felt then sore and bitter)

      swiveling my torso down into the hole I've dug
      I resolve to wait it out

here on the hill until the money
proof of my goodness

      makes up its mind to return to me
      I hum to myself as night comes on   and swear to stay with it   nestling close
            into the shelter of the great rock

the Big Dipper and the Little Dipper still know where to find me, I think
I am in my bunker, like him, waiting for the final—

      not so bad after all the waiting
      in the bunker I realize it was not the money I had buried

but the bodies, those bodies really I had buried
so what I had meant to do had been done, and what I had meant to find

      had been found: the mulch about their ankles, the sweat dripping down from
            their pyramids
      the one eye on the pyramid, green   lifting away from the bricked-in base—

I am in my bunker, waiting

I wanted that death and so

my major and I

outside the cellar window frame, white-paned (outside the cellar window pane,
    white-framed)

      the snow the snow lies low upon the ground a white thought covering covering
      at least that is what it seems to sing

through the white-framed pane we see the daffodils
the daffodils, oh, they have come too soon

      outside the cellar window, the bed   the garden bed
      the snow the snow lies low upon the ground a white thought covering

    *

after school and after supper sometimes I go out in the back yard to listen to the pilgrims
the pilgrims who were here a century and a century and a century before

      they fall in stagnant pools and tie their buckles, shut the buckles on their craniums
      the wilderness is fearful, but at night they close up tight their ventricles

listen to the wind howl about their houses the houses of their antinomies
caution the wind   level the gun   and bring the mind to slaughter

      of savagery which lies always like a faithful companion below the lintel
      of illumination

this is what I learn in school and from the oaks, which with their boughs
are always teaching me, teaching me

    *

and I go out into the back yard
not into the secret garden but into the secret game reserve

      where I enclose the unicorn if only I could find it I keep waiting, I keep waiting
      for its arrival and sit for many days and hours despondent at its non-arrival

and make many deals with divinity negotiations with non-being
which at this age is the very best friend to me   that if it comes

       I will—give something—non-specified but definite—a great
       sacrifice—I perhaps should have specified because I keep waiting

and waiting into the small hours of the night by the great rock
(in the near woods) I had designated my protector. I keep waiting

       and feel I cannot leave, really, until some sort of sign has been given.
       these are often not preordained and therefore all the more difficult

to designate, tag, and bag (capture). oh, how I want it! I keep waiting,
digging down into the leaves by the great rock, down into my bivouac

       knowing certainly I am following someone's orders
       even if I cannot see them.

       *

I keep saying to my companion, the major
by me, that if we just wait one more minute—(and then the next,

       and then the next)—shall appear—right around this corner—
       a beautiful beast, which is a great love, to hold into our interior

its thick and spiraling entirety—a culmination. and so we keep waiting,
the major and I, who also has begun to slip into non-being—he started

       with a leg, and then an arm, and I comforted him by saying, What's an amputation
       here and there, I have lost more in an afternoon than I care to say. it's best to lose

a lot before the meal of noonday and then the evening redounds in calm solicitude.
the major lies still and quiet right beside me, for we share a sleeping sack, to warn

       against the chill. I blow on his hand. (I love my major.) he says, Hadn't we better
       be getting in, corporal? (I am no corporal, dear reader, but that is what he calls
          me, dear.)

and we both look up over the brink of the hill and through the wood to the house,
which glows warm and yellow with its culture and its burning logs. so near!

> I hold up the plastic laminated sheet which enscrolls our orders (it is
>   invisible), and take
> a look. put a finger on the transparent line, the exact date and time of—
>   I don't think

I'd better read that to you, dear major, I say. No, that's fine, he says, for he is a
    patient
man, and kind. (he is not a fatalist, like I—) we snuggle. without that extra arm,

> he is the easier to hold. we look back at the house, from which spires of smoke
> have begun to unfurl. Look, there's animals, we say. and we begin to count

them, making of it a game: a smoke cloud in shape of a—

> ✶

and there the lion biting the back of the bull, and there the leopard
attacking the long-horned caprid

> there the lions unfurling beside the temple door
> and there the human-headed winged bull

there mosaiced, the orange-maned lion, striding amidst gods and kings
down the great processional way

> dragons and bulls alternating about the great gate
> there the leaping stag, there the necklace of the ringing doves

there the calypso of old, sea-streaming, there the leopard all in carnelian
there the gate of the watcher, there the hierophant

> we watch the smoke rising from the house in shapes of animals, and make
> a game of naming them. the house, in the night disappearing, or seeming to.

the house in the night (white, green-
shuttered) devolving in fumes of—

⁂

    we hold ourselves to it, committed, to the great rock we have chosen,
    or has been chosen, a sort of bulwark. meanwhile my major, slowly,

begins to go—first a shoulder, then a clavicle. a groin is my great loss—
it has been my comfort, innocent—with its inner thigh, its toe.

    his lips go also, dear reader, and his curved cheekbones.
    I cry then, reader. soon all I remain beside

is a disencumbered entrail. I say my prayers to it,
I sing to it in the night all the songs I know, by heart

    and even before knowing, I give to it all that I have ever
    known or shall ever know or hope to know, suck all that out

of the great undulating universes swirling round about and in
us, sing—I draw it up, sing all that to it, my entrail.

⁂

    my little entrail sweet beside me, faithful.
    I kiss it, I do, my little entrail

path switchbacking carefully on a wooded hill
from side to side. little labyrinth,

    into which A. descended, with only his pluck
    and no map, to stalk the minotaur who,

apprised of the arrival, seeing it in the foresight gifted
to bulls, grieved in his heart to have to kill it,

such a beautiful boy, so full of courage and earnestness,
but kill it he would have to, for this was his labyrinth,

built by Daedalus at the behest of him—for each bull
needs its labyrinth, the underground path of knowing

where the shadow falls across and illumines, the gate
into the vestibule of *terra,* territoriality, terror

torrentiality, terrific atlases of falling precipices,
iced in cataracts, desert temblors.

*

it is thus. I see it so, and wish I had not seen.
I hold my major, then

I hold him, press him, brother, entrail, against my ventral
surfaces, smear him—careful, reverent—against my belly.

and I know it to be good, though it looks not.

I gather down into my leaves about me, there below the great rock,
which somehow offers shelter, as I lie amidst the keening mulch

(and weep, and weep, and weep)
my heart, half-broken, not the less the ardent

I wanted that death and so

I wanted that death and so
I called to it

       I called to it and I called to it
       from across the waters

finally obedient
it comes to us

       and the fire from the tower
       rains down

upon my head
where reverent I have assembled

       in the desert where we began
       once and now begin

and Aeneas comes upon the flaming city

and Aeneas comes upon the flaming city

by the time I awaken the city already is burning
I join in battle knowing the city already as good as fallen

      a warrior can yet make a show of it and make his might
      known to the world

for it is how one dies that is in the end most vital

      on my shoulder I carry the weight of my father
      who only with great solicitude can I persuade to leave after all

for he argues he has led a fine life and should be let to end it as he chooses
I carry him on my shoulder, great infant, out of the burning city

      by the time I awaken the city already is burning

and the walls impregnable of centuries are falling

I say to them: the gates are open
and the city walls impregnable of centuries are falling

    I am no longer a fortress   no longer are you
    I sing of warfare and a man at war

and Aeneas comes upon the flaming city
(and, for just a moment—)

Aeneas in the oval office

I have made a great war and I shall do it again
the war some days it goes best with vermouth

      I find the odor of the dead magnificent
      I like best how they exist in pieces

on my desk I keep one such remnant   an unfleshed skull
cogitus cogitandum as the ancients said   to remind me how to think

I preside over a celestial realm strewn with drifts of dunes which, in my dream,
     slowly slide into the sea
in the meantime I am aloft them, riding, riding

      I am walking to Gallipoli
      I see you also are walking   I do my best to avoid you

when you were my age did you ever wonder
what time the stars made to go to bed at night?

      I thought the stars might have difficulty sleeping because of themselves so
         ambient
      due to this I pitied them

I think often of collapse
first the veins then the ventricles then the vessels of the mercantile

      you say, but the mercantile is long past
      I was not briefed on this shift and so will not acknowledge it

in my dreams there is often collapse
beneath a starboard sail   beneath a twelve-gallon hat

      but I was not born to be the ruin of anything
      I am new renewed and renewing

everywhere I touch there grows a towering plant
scarce root in the desert

in my dreams there is often collapse
I am walking toward a future which I cannot yet see   a massif overtowering
    me

this dream however counters my theme
of inviolable inviolability   and so far and wide I do not advertise it

    in my dreams often I must look in a mirror in which it appears my teeth the
        front ones are rotting

this would not happen in real life   for I am gifted with the finest dentist
and so I awaken   completely at ease

    I am aloft in my beneficence
    and am not unknown to majesty   the multitude awaits me

I have made a great war and I shall do it again
and the multitude awaits me

Aeneas & the pilgrim child set out into the city

I shall build a city upon a hill
and upon a hill and upon a hill and upon a hill

> I am a little shepherd piping low
> through the valleys of Babylon

I shall build a city upon a hill
and it shall be as a light unto—

> and upon a hill and upon a hill and upon a hill a citadel—
> *the world*   I shall build

through the valleys of Babylon
I lay down and weep

> *I lay down and weep*
> *and weep   for thee, Babylon*

but then I, I recall I—
I am aloft in my omnipotence

> and so there is no problem

I think I do not know that Europe

I think I do not know that Europe
it is not in me or of me or because of me

        it is not waiting for me to return
        it does not remember

when it held me inside it
Europa during the long banks of winter

        no I was never there
        was never there

the seacoasts sing their green cliffsongs without me
howl their long pitchgreens down the incline spit of the sea

        I am unnecessary
        no I was never there

no high keening songs await to be sung
by such a one as me

        no pause between notes
        in the stone-brooked wail

where I jump in   it is complete
sufficient unto itself

        and when I sing it is in low tones
        past hearing

over drifts of sand come I

I am a little pilgrim child
over the drifts come I

      over the seas journey to build
      a city upon a hill

I am a little pilgrim child
the ways call out with means

      the leopard to the lion plains
      sharp joy to the mountain screams

I am a little pilgrim child
my antelope is fawning

      I'd give a kingdom for a hilt
      its gun has got bright dawning

I am a little pilgrim child
I have a journey to make

      Gethsemane—trembling—garden
      long night for your sake

and a one-ton bomb named Moab
tilts over Baghdad

in these months we wait for eruptions

in these months, we wait for eruptions to begin across another's sky.
the haiku artist has long ago ceased using season-words in the promontory line.

> early February, nighttime, slow stream of planes across our sky
> unhurried, domestic. behind, green flushes of growth.

a ringing in the ear of the giant who sits just outside the window blinds.
a poplar composes its capacious speeches, altered by the rumor of the room, blue
    box of light.

> elsewhere, I hear, on other continents,
> they are standing in lines to buy gas masks.

as for us, we stroll about the upper world
free   and uncontrolled

they say the war has begun over there

they tell me the war has begun over there
it is in all the news reports   a jubilant static

      in the fields next to the house   the night birds are chirping
      in the tall grasses I hear them

and I go out to walk in it in the war

      I can smell it in the magnolias
      and in the grey buds, just swollen, of the pussy willows

there is a breeze from off the ocean
and this also, inexplicably, seems to carry it

      I walk on and on in the night   ascending to the crest of the hill
      where dwells a circle of pines, tall Montereys, broad-boughed

in the deep darkness amidst them I smell it
alive in the electric-strung city

      onward I scent it in the narcissi   just fulgent by the curb's new green
      and in the overhanging branches

within I hear ringing out cries of joy
oh, a cause for celebration, it is said

      some approach and say, Do not worry, for we have it on the surest
      intelligence   the intelligence of the greatest of nations

and I go out to walk in it   the great dream of the nation
palpable as the magnolias

      and I feel it in the night then
      and something else just beginning

(and I reach out and, pulling a bare petal
I touch, I touch it to my tongue)

these are the days of nothing but triumph

these days are the days of nothing but triumph.
at midday one receives from across the courtyard

      the pure announcement of the campanile
      melody rising and descending   redoubtable

cheerful fugue
for an audience of choristers

      only later after a pause
      the low-toned knelling of the hour

blimmmmb   blimmmmb   blimmmmb   blimmmmb

      these days each day is the prelude to the dinning of the campanile
      each front page clattering, *Victory is always, Victory is here*

I am a little pilgrim child

I am a little pilgrim child
over drifts of sand come I

over the seas journey to build
a city upon a hill

here inside as of old the sandbox

Aeneas in the airport

in the airport I see Aeneas from a distance
Aeneas has her helmet on

     it is white and smudged from a distance
     the helmet of Aeneas

smudged with the light
of the desert

     I touch her arm
     Where are you off to? I ask her

I'm with the National Guard, she says
I'm off to Iraq

     Don't worry, she says, and touches my arm
     I will keep you safe   you can rest at home in that knowledge

       Right, I say, Thank you

I watch Aeneas with the others board her plane
Charlottesville to Fallujah

     I say a quick, involuntary prayer for her and for the others
     (although I am not a prayer   and never have been)   and then she's off

Aeneas boards her plane
tall, she has to duck her head to enter

     the white-smudged helmet hits the frame of the entrance
     and she takes it off, that spiked helmet

holding it instead against her heart
for the duration

I am at my stance in Basra

I am at my stance in Basra
in the morning as I have been ordered

in the morning as I have been ordered
I take up my position, defensive, in the masjid

I do each thing quite carefully
in the morning I kneel in the morning

in the dust which reflects
the arbor of the street

I kneel in the dust which knows also
beyond the street the last glance of the dome

below me I grind with my knee the dust
which remembers still—just beyond the dome—

the slanting, the slipping light— (home)

here inside as of old the sandbox

     I made a god
     I made a god
     I made it out of clay

I made a god
I made a god
in six hundred and thirteen days

     I made a god
     I made a god
     and put it in the soil to play

but that fence-lot god
it talked so loud
I couldn't hear anything else

     and so I had to turn it off
     once again without a god
     here inside as of old the sandbox

america I think may be a kind of codeword

america I think may be a kind of codeword
for just what I am not sure

    but trying to detect it
    I go about the earth

actually I do not go about the earth but sit instead
here at my little table

    and I listen to the war
    on the radio

where is the war?

where is the war? is the war in the ampules
of the morning dew, globules

      whole and peaceful? or is the war rather
      in the lavender geodes cut open on the jeweler's

counter? does the war live in the classroom, children
pacing out slow textbooks? where is the war?

      is it in the overriding calm of this morning,
      what one always refuses to tell?

does it live, this war, in one hundred thousand
commuters, each sheathed in her metal, gliding

      glissando, fearing no danger?

no, our war is elsewhere.
for we have determined it so.

      and when I wake, I can't hear you
      for the roar of the clouds

the dropping of dawn
on the unsuspecting   city

the war it writes me a letter

lately I am making my way toward the war
for it has a great need for me

I know because it wrote me a letter telling me so
and the fertile crescent has never been so dear to me

yes the war it wrote me a letter
in which the following:

War Progress Administration
District of the Capitol
The Desert, the Desert D.C.

Dear Patron of the Arts / Dear Patron of Infinity,

We have a great need of you here. You might not think so, but it is true. For it has a need for all types, the war, for the war, it is capacious.

The committee, after having reviewed your oeuvre, has detected in it a distinct preference for the theme of death.

This work site would offer a great deal of field experience for the young poet struggling between the ideal and the real.

Consider carefully this opportunity to deepen your portfolio. Rest not upon the ink-stained pillow.

Moreover, we see fit to mention that for years—based upon the proof of your diaries—you have yearned for the mantle of the "engaged writer."

We leave you, then, with one final question: Who more engaged than the soldier?

Respectfully yours,

the war

soon I shall be making my way toward the war
I walk slowly into the field where I await myself

freedom is walking itself on a leash

and I am myself war

1. and I am myself war

2. when I arise in the morning I like to think to myself *but I am not in the war* I am in the war

3. letter to a young _____

4. and I am myself war

a sheaf of war

a sheaf of war
I find myself at the top of an enormous umbel

       tip of the tsunami
       it carries me

freedom is walking itself on a leash

freedom is walking itself on a leash
across the great courtyard of the century

    it can't recall who it has bound
    and who it has freed

and so it proceeds
regarding everyone

    equally as culpable
    as itself

great palaces beckon
it enters them

    *

knowing it might have a bit of shame about it, but adoring really
the striding about the stately galleries of princes

    delightful fountains spewing in the arc of midday   rows of glass cases
    filled with ballroom gowns, many-tiered, some in shimmering teal

and the ribbons, colors slightly greyed,
of mustachioed warriors on display

    *

and outside in the backyard, there
where the men are smoking and attending to the patrol

    of their hand-held playstations
    here are the gardens of Nebuchadnezzar

oh, it gives one a fine sense of history
as if the psalms were standing upright in the air

    I kneel in the morning   I kneel
    in the reflected dust

freedom is walking itself on a leash
across the great avenue/little road of the desert

    it can't remember who it has tied to its throat
    and who it has shuttered

into the cage
of the clattering sky

    I kneel in the morning   I kneel
    in the dust reflected from—

freedom is walking itself on a leash
it can't recall who it has tied

    to the little half-loops of its closehairs
    warmed by the scent of the animal body

building the pyramid   on the currency
I kneel I kneel in—

    freedom is walking itself on a leash
    across a place it now declares it has

come to by accident
—instance of missed intelligence—

    and when I get to the river—
    and when I get to the river—

freedom is walking itself on a leash
and when it gets to the river it lies down

    almost as if as if
    as if it were forgetting itself

the visitor pays a visit to the Statue of Liberty

the visitor pays a visit to the Statue of Liberty

I climb up the hundreds of stairs
up, up into your breasts, oh America

      I touch them, I do, from the inside
      the great swelling earth-mounds of you

I look out upon the book you are holding
(the words, I cannot read them from here)

      the plains of the states before us—this openness I love, oh America
      the tour group, jostling for the best picture, brushes past

would you allow me, oh America, to sequester
in you but for a moment more?

      for I have loved my time within you, dear one
      I admit, yes—I have loved you.

I lean my neck now out and up, up toward your flame
with so much force you heft it, oh darling

      torch scorched up into the half-night of the sky
      trick of the light (or is it sunset we see in it?)

the security guards have come to the landing
I put my pocket camera away

      (did I mention that I loved you, loved
      how you took me in?—generous bosom)

they are calling the time, they are calling
the last elevator down

      (and so I thank you once more for having allowed
      me to stay here within you)

and it is now—glancing up at your diadem—
oh she of the seven spires—each ray

      spinning out its glass shard
      upon the waiting swells—

from your pale skull I see your crown unloose
from its temples, lift, celestial, weighted discus—

              passing over the waters—

                    toward the expanse to the east

      (and moves over me a sentiment of
      would it be too much to say misery)

I am led by the guardians
shivering   away from the vista

      down into the elevator, moving down within you
      and I plummet to the very depths

           of you, oh America

when I get to the bottom of the city I cry out

ample upon the painted sands

from inside the body of the horse
we look out upon those who owe us obeisance

    soon I shall be what I am made

on my shield I paint a bright maiden
sometimes in the desert I lie awake

    ample upon the painted sands
    I think I must have walked here

I claim a greater place for this place
I will teach them how to be themselves

    I remember the code Babylonian
    incised upon the tablets of Hammurabi

I cannot say I do not often have my doubts
but doubt is not the best builder of character

    I am an orthodox innovator

I consider doubt even a bit immoral
and so I wipe it from my ignominy

when I get to the bottom of the city I cry out

when I get to the bottom of the city I cry out
as if that even might help me

    I become to myself unwieldy
    and begin to think I might no longer carry me

but I have made a vow to sing myself
and to be others when myself can no longer be me

    I have made a vow to sing myself
    and to sing the body republic

and to sing the body of the body of the body
replicating in its unerring mastery

    yes I have made a vow to sing myself
    and being here can see no other place to be

I have counted greatly it might be said on there being always others who might
    recall my exploits
who would sing them on their broadsheets out loud into a dawn into a dawn
    upon a screen of a history

    knowing this I am not afraid no not ever
    indeed I fear   for nothing

take great faith in my walks by the river
the Potomac alike with the Tigris

    bear only my head downward
    knowing for certain the outcome shall only be upward

I lead my people into a dome gold-foiled

and I lead my people thus
into a dome gold-foiled I have foreshadowed

     I lead them   and the faithful are faithful
     and shall be duly rewarded   in their heaven as in mine

and if outward is not my destiny
I do not know what else shall be   for the republic is great within me

     if a border is not where I find my retreat
     I would find it instead in these entrails

I take myself a tour of Nineveh

and I take myself a tour of the embattled country
where the people have been sleeping a long sleep

       I awaken them with my solvent touch
       and tell them: Hassan is here! Hassan of the seven seas!

they bend down to my robes' gilded ordure   so beside themselves are they
it causes some to spit or drool, loosen upon garments wobbling globules

       I know what it is to be beside myself and so I feel honestly some sort
       of alliance with them   however of the moment or fleeting

they welcome me into their homes (got this on film, you can see)
for I am Hassan   Hassan of the seven seas

       it was as if for a moment I were really and completely—
       which I had not been, no, not for a very long time

and I take myself a tour of Nineveh   many beautiful artifacts abounding
I tip my hat to them   for I am golden and arisen

       they feel they do these honest folk the wonder of war
       and who has not found it so?

Interrogation #2356

Interrogation #2356

SCENE: INTERROGATOR, two GUARDS, and a PRISONER.

INTERROGATOR (*Addresses* GUARDS.) Bring him please out of his cell. Tell him to— (*Stops.*) The translator has not yet arrived. Wait a moment, please, for the translator.

TRANSLATOR *arrives.*

(*Continues.*) Very well, then. (*Addresses* TRANSLATOR.) Tell him to ask him the question that was asked of him yesterday. The one about the—

TRANSLATOR *says something.*

He knows. Don't think that he doesn't know because his file clearly shows that—an involvement with—it is documented. I simply want him to say—on the details we are not quite clear yet. That is, we have details, we want him to know, and we want to build upon the strength of that, meanwhile make him want to give the details we do not yet have, not advertising the not yet as a lack exactly—a strategy. (*Stops explaining, commands.*) Don't translate that.

TRANSLATOR *asks a question.*

The "make him want"? Just wait, you'll see. (Eyeing prisoner, quick aside to TRANSLATOR.) How long have you been on the island? (*Doesn't wait for answer, turning to fully face the* PRISONER.)

(*Begins again.*) Ask him about Transakastan, the place behind the caves where—ask him.

(*Responds to* TRANSLATOR.) This? (INTERROGATOR *gestures toward her garments.*) Form fitting—it bends to him. (*Faces* PRISONER *again.*) I will need to describe the predicament in which I find—like this:

(*To* PRISONER.) My breasts—you can see—firm with wanting.

(*To* TRANSLATOR, *still facing* PRISONER.) It is a procedure.

(*To* PRISONER.) My nipples—you can see—tight as minarets.

(*To* TRANSLATOR.) Go ahead—proceed.

(*To* PRISONER.) I've been thinking about you all night. That's right. Look at me—it's true, you can see it.

(*To* GUARDS and TRANSLATOR.) Now, please stand to the side.

(*To* TRANSLATOR.) It is perhaps peculiar to see me like this. Here it is *de rigueur.* You can look it up. Strictures, a procedure. The thong? An instrument of compliance.

(*As if to self.*) The smear I leave on him could be my own.

(*Abruptly, to* TRANSLATOR.) The women back home where he's from? Wouldn't give him anything like—

(*Quickly, now, to* PRISONER.) I've been thinking about you all night in my bed.

(*Again, as if to self.*) That's right. I could be my own translator. (*Quietly, to someone, unspecified.*) Wait now.

(*To* GUARDS.) Get him up from the chair—he can see better. (This has to come off.)

(*To* TRANSLATOR, *or self.*) Bit cold in here.

(*Addresses* PRISONER.) You see, I could put it in me. (*Waits.*) Tell him, now, quick, to look at me. (*Waits, briefly, staring intently.*) Why won't he look—if only he would look—it would be quicker and—

(*Now, again, to* PRISONER, *as if in song.*) Prisoner, prisoner, now you are come to me. I cannot stop touching myself as I look at you looking at me as you see I—it is wet now with your—it is yours, you made it. This. Scent. Of copper. On my fingers, on your nostrils, quickly now across your waiting brow your—your stubble, quick with ruin.

(*Breathless, half-triumphant, half-crestfallen.*) It is just so.

(*Again, frustrated.*) I want—if only he would—

(*To* GUARDS.) Bend him down again. (*Hears something.*) Just wait.

(*To the assembled company.*) What did he say?

(*Is told by* TRANSLATOR *and/or* GUARDS.)

(*Again addresses* PRISONER.) Prostitute. Mmmm.

(*To all, while still looking at* PRISONER.) Well, I'd like to see how he gets clean tonight.

(*To* GUARDS, TRANSLATOR.) Alright, tell him he can go.

(*To* TRANSLATOR, *tone reassuring, chipper, excited. They walk out of the room together.*) He's alright, it was ink. It'll make him think twice about his silence, perhaps. I think he just might turn toward us. With a bit more pressure. Tomorrow, you and I, we'll press onward. You could probably use some rest. (*Turning to* TRANSLATOR, *brightly.*) How long have you been on the island?

you, there, back behind beginning

in the end you implode me

I too am behind a wall
a great sea separates me from you

        something dark about your face
        but I cannot see you

you too thought it would be this way
but I   never

        when we walked to the wall you were crying
        but I   never

and you you were the one who said   a sky
before I—could say anything

        the buddhas of Bamiyan imploded
        but a thousand are born each day

you there before beginning
you before ever

        I too thought we might marry
        we had never met   this was a complication

in the end you implode me
as I walk calmly about the street

        looking down once again at my entrails
        red-gold labyrinth

this after all was all I had wished
some kind of beginning   meretricious

I have met the enemy and—

I have met the enemy in the café
into my bed has slipped the enemy

>   from behind, it gathers an arm about my waist.
>   slowly and surely, knowing exactly its way, it—

my enemy is astonished by and cannot stop
admiring my great girth

>   I am so large to it   I fill its dreams
>   my enemy is absolutely enamored of me

each and every day the enemy thinks of me
superimposed am I upon its skull.

>   in February the enemy begins elaborate plans
>   for the day of Saint Valentine

how it shall gift and reward me
the enemy composes songs for me

>   it doesn't have much, my enemy,
>   but it wants to give to me

according to the ancient rules of generosity:
gift to the giver, gift to the received.

>   in internet cafés the enemy and I make our trysts
>   prearranged by coordinated assignation

(for they—*they*—must never know)

>   when one day I begin to question the basis of its commitment,
>   affect modesty, citing my gargantuan

proportions, it reassures me,
Oh, but all the more to love of you!

in the bed the enemy comes up behind me,
its haunches close on   perfectly we seem to fit.

(and yet, my enemy is very, very little.
sometimes it almost is lost in me.)

to our great surprise, the enemy and I
are able to link fleeing sperm to flinching egg

soon we make an appointment with the doctor and the forceps of death
and set at the same time the birth announcement

together we shall make many children, fat
some of them meager, for all that

by now, it must be admitted, many others have fallen away in their stated
affections for me   practicing their spurious, predictable actions

and yet my enemy still, after all these years
sends love-notes   in hidden envelopes

by the *caché* nature of our love
I am of it more certain

it always keeps me—my dear, my enemy—guessing

I have met the enemy and—
I have met the enemy and—

I search in you my own destruction

I search in you my own destruction
what veil has come between us cannot be

    becoming and unbecoming
    unbecoming and becoming

infidel, infidel, infidel, I—
and I want with a wanting of wanting

when smoke arises from the tube car nostrils

when smoke arises from the tube car nostrils
we are cast into darkness

    another's gut adorns your sleeve
    we are hundreds of feet below our own thoughts

the evasive tactics of living are showcasing themselves
many hours pass in a technique of cells

    and no one comes   after screams we talk amongst ourselves
    shuddered in a row of shoulders shadowed

for no reason I put my hand against a window
it finds a bit I think of entrail

    at least what it feels like only from touch
    I wish I had—absurd—taken the bus

in the darkness I look into my hand
as usual unforeseeable

    a rock skitters outside and one imagines it
    an advent a rescue a soldier

treading down the cavern toward us
in hope a woman calls out, Some are dying here.

    silence.

with memory of surface am I concerned
impenetrate the one-eyed integral

I wake up to become my own terrorist

in the dream I am walking along the avenue where—
in the dream I wake up as my terrorist

      a chaos born of the four winds and a wanting
      entropy entropy I am falling toward myself

metamorphoses and truncations, truncations and metamorphoses

      the sun was in the star, or the star was in the sun
      slovenly slovenly I am walking along

in the dream I wake up to become my terrorist

I walk slowly into the field where I await myself

I walk slowly into the field where I await myself
you are there also but I cannot see you

    it is a field of avenues
    it is a field of daily

and there also a deep avarice which I have birthed

    still I stand silently
    in wait for me

bellum omnium contra omnes

bellum omnium contra omnes bellum omnium contra omnes bellum omnium contra
omnes bellum omnium contra omnes bellum omnium contra omnes bellum omnium

   bellum omnium contra omnes   the war of all against all
   unabashedly I immerse myself   in the blood that derives from blossoms

      there is no tragedy that cannot acquit itself
      of the red printing on the walls of the subway car

   across my knees I admire your script
   slanting down the side of a face   pockmarked of an epoch

      and I stare into the plaza of a lap
      someone shall break the unbreakable glass

   hands, written-on, climb up—

      and I repeat my punctuation
      a kind of comforting

bellum omnium contra omnes bellum omnium contra omnes bellum omnium contra
omnes bellum omnium contra omnes bellum omnium contra omnes bellum omnium

I hope you don't mind if I wiretap you

I hope you don't mind if I wiretap you
I do it only so as better to know you

    terribly terribly tapping and tapping
    terribly terribly tapping

I do it only so as better to know you
who can say now   I do not listen?

    timorous, timorous, give me your little wrist
    darling you hear I'm listening

terribly terribly tapping

    I do it, you see, to embrace you, my dear
    the lurk in the dark   the tree of the guard

I do it to keep from you what might happen
the trick in the night before god

    tappingly tappingly tapping

crossing New York Harbor by ferry

crossing New York Harbor by ferry

oh America, a visitor once again, I look out the windows from your crown
and it is as if forever I have known you.

> having climbed the stairs—355—I counted—to reside within you
> I dwell within, speak now from within you.

>> *

it is not infrequently, and especially in moments such as these, I am reminded
of the days when you, you were my first girlfriend, oh America

> the one whose hand I took only in the dark

upon the shuttered road, the road shuttered in night
in the alley of forgetting, for this is where I think I must have found you, oh
> America

> I, the discoverer—forget all those rosters of intruders—
> only I who found the true you in you.

>> *

oh America, in whom I breathe sullenly just now.
the tour guide is too loud, my dear, she would ruin the bright music

> I remember of you, my personal soundtrack to my knowing of you
> do you know what I mean, oh dear?

that song, playing in you, it was there and with that moment
repeated of song that I came to know you, I think it was summer—

> I think it might have been the summer when, after much hand-holding
> you allowed me—furtively, was it?—to enter into you truly

first I think only with my fingers, oh America, you liked that—
and didn't I ask permission first? to enter? I recall you breathing

that I need not ask, so great was your need to have me in you,
I believe that I had held off, desiring brusque, frontational

over the great and torrid surfaces of you, oh alabaster maiden
how hot you became, that summer! or was it winter indeed—

yes, with the fingers, was how you liked it at first, oh America
I need not mention—I am too polite—how wet you were

oh, a veritable walrus, mustachioed, of wetness!
a good song, you are a good music to me.

*

it didn't pause there. what did I feel there, inside you?
I felt—with my fingertips—for the occasion I had clipped

my nails, a gesture perhaps of braggadocio that yet proved
worthy of the moment—I found—with my fingertips—

inside you—it was not so like a well as I had imagined it might well
be, not so cylindrical, nor so evenly spherical or even trapezoidal

not so pure-plane geometry, you were rather, I found—in the center
of you—the route of you was uneven, America, a trajectory, lapsed

tongue tilted to one side, a children's carnival ride that pitches from wall
to padded wall, under the feet always leaning, nearing, lurching, leering—

responsive you were, America—to me—not a simulation of a game
but such a reality—oh, America, such a reality—how you surprised me!

I was almost unprepared, America, I must admit this now, I said nothing of it then
of course. I was—I would never have said—I—and now, also my intent

is not to be salacious, I hope you do not feel it that way, America, as I stand
now, feet firmly planted, and speak from within you:

I felt promised to you. we had not been betrothed—I felt sure your father
though I had not met him, would have none of me. it was rumored

he lived in Alaska, in the Yukon, in the gold and then the oil fields
sitting on the ice, in the dark, hour after hour, month after month

    to preclude the looting of his hoard, stroking his long, grey, still-agile beard.
    no, I did not want to meet with him! we were not betrothed

this was not even spoken of, between you and me, dear America
in the dark there, while I kept myself

    warm inside your lurching cunt. oh, your great cunt, dear America!
    may I speak of it? it is only with the—I assure you—the greatest of respect,
        dear America

that I lay out here my praise to your towering, ever-great cunt.
oh, the inroads and the outroads of your cunt, the hidden corners of your cunt

    the Route 66 of your cunt, the round-that-bend-and-around-the-corner-
    finds-you-a-diner of your cunt, the backroads, the moonshine-still recipes
        of your cunt

the frolicsome, winsome nature of your cunt—so sweet, and—
how many peoples I met in there, they are so friendly, the peoples

    of America, that can be said of them, so good-natured
    so kind, they would pull out a chair and turn back a bed for you in their
        own homes

so generous and bosom-hearted are they, the peoples of America
who I met there in those times, deep in the inroads of your tender cunt, oh dear
    America.

    such a trusting time, those times, when first I knew you, dear America.
    not that anything has changed, no, I wouldn't say that. you can still sense that,

deep within them, within the dark shadow of mistrust, an upwelling of native
ingenuity and genuine, rolling, icy creek of trust. they want that, I think, America.

   ✶

  don't they? as for the remainder of the liaison, America, perhaps I will not here
  speak of it, oh dear. let us keep it within us, dear America.

how I lay with you night after night, how you spoke, some Scheherazade—
just who were you keeping alive, you or me?—how you spoke your slow shadows

  into the arc of my chest, not daring to meet my eyes, even, as you divulged
  night after night, your deeds, past and future—for even the future

ones you sought forgiveness in my chest—your crown (you were not yet, no not
  on that night
wearing your helmet, had not yet donned it) came up just under my chin

  and your stray locks tickled at my clavicle, my exposed nape of skin; yes,
  sought forgiveness, and I let these thoughts rest in the open

space that exists between all lovers, the pause between the stellar interstices;
not answering quickly or easily, but letting these rest,

  like our then-shared breath, between us.

   ✶

  I loved you then, America.

dearly. beyond myself. beyond reason.
is that not the way of all first loves?

  I loved you then, America.
  Has anything changed? you ask.

I would not answer hastily.
the view, slightly different, from here.

the crowds, jostling about me, perhaps a little less fervent.
the expanse over Manhattan a bit more open,

perhaps this is only an illusion, brought by the reflection of the glass
off the giant front of the outpost of the North Face.

I thank you, America, for letting me rest so inside you,
if but for another moment. your moments come more and more

close between, or is it farther. I won't make
anything of that, I'll leave it to you.

*

isn't it crazy? yes, a crazy love, faded, though, a bit now. would you permit me,
dear, a few words of the ex-lover, even of advice,

if it would not offend you overmuch? then, alright, these:
Take hold of yourself, dear America, as I have.

if I might say it, you are more than your philosophy
perhaps has permitted. I believe in you, oh America.

please hear this with all the tenderness of one
who has loved you deeply. you and I, both enduring

and I have a dream that,
though separate, we might still do it

touch, decently
from within our inner

recesses

oh America, my dear
and for what was between us

I do
now grieve

*

I take the stairs now—the long way down—passing through
the solid body again of you, descending, descending

in you, almost in love, as ever, with you.

there are echoes in the stairs, but perhaps that is your open book
shaking in the wind of a Northeaster, or perhaps it is merely

the shadow of a great and labored breathing.

reaching the ground again of the island,
crossing in the ferry to the mainland.

over there, returning, I'll get a warm drink
and shake it all off—the memories, the past

the present, the future—or perhaps not.
I'll write an entry in my journal, I think

signing it with both of our names, written doubly
leaning into the edifices of one another

pierced with the constant and shuddering
flame of our love, as if we had known each other

always and in a past life, a life
bound always to this one in which we lie.

finally I am the star of my own beheading video

why didn't the flowers?

why didn't the flowers apologize?
which diary was the one I grew?

yesterday morning I believe you blew
yourself up for my country—

because of it, I mean.
I wait and listen

to the wind hitting through the flag.
one blue sky derides another.

even the hungry grass remembers
how to lift a gross flank

toward the sun, just up
over the yardarm,

ancient measure, now unmeasured, like the tone
of voice in which you speak to me.

I shy away, I shy away,
even while my own clothes sail off and linger

above the drifts of tin. why didn't
the flowers apologize?

discourse on impossibility

the deer have come out from the hills
into our yards and have eaten our blossoms

      we want to shoot them or at least scatter them, teach
      them a lesson. it's not their nibbling snouts we see

nor their cottontail rumps
but the impossibility of their wants.

      those animals would have us cede what we have already bought
      with a currency they fail to recognize.

in the middle of the wall we built lies a picture
window, and in the middle of the picture

      window lies the harbor, frame for nubbed
      Mount Tamalpais, nature low-lying, distant, shrubbed.

tanks also muscle across grandmothers,
in the distance, across old brothers.

      everywhere power is mistaken for power,
      and the mighty suffer with the angry.

finally I am the star of my own beheading video

finally I am the star of my own beheading video
I have come a long way for this

>   the other characters
>   are quite realistic actors

as well as directors
for they have prepared my script

>   from which I attempt
>   not to diverge

for I imagine still if only I promise—
(I lean into the microphone)

>   I speak into the camera and beg for the life you and
>   I   lived together once

and I do hope
you will do everything in your power to

>   to meet the demands of the insurgents   of the
>   insurgence   of the insurgence

blindfolded now and alone
I speak into the microphone

>   the view from here is lustrous
>   finally I appear in the beheading video

I imagine now what shall be cut from what
and here I disclose it to you:

>   my tender Florida cut from my Dakota
>   my private Dakota cut from my Nevada

my Nevada cut from my Seattle
my Seattle cut from my antipodes

    my antipodes cut from my Albuquerque
    my Albuquerque cut from my New Jersey

my New Jersey cut from my Alleghenies
my Alleghenies cut from my Park Slope

    my Park Slope cut from my Alabama
    my Alabama cut from my El Camino Real

my El Camino Real cut from my Mission
and my mission cut from my—

    and this I do not know I do not witness
    you will have to send me a note   send it to my home address

I know that the breastplate shall sever
I guess that the gullet shall crack

    I hope that the throat will be left standing
    until it can crawl its way home from—

I know that the throat will dream a phantom body
and the body dream a phantom lake above itself

    finally I am the star of my own beheading video
    the other characters are quite realistic actors

and they take direction well
for I am preparing our script

and Aeneas appears on the reality show

and Aeneas appears on the reality show

she arrives on set with the form
of her best beloved warrior

    laid out upon his shield
    as makeup sessions spin

she kneels by the corpse upon the shield
and begins to speak   out her remembrances

    the art director approaches, touches her on the arm
    Ah, I'm not sure that's very, you know, "true to life"

Yes, says Aeneas, you are right

    after a few episodes it is deemed that she
    is an inappropriate contestant

character lacking
in sufficient realism

    artfully the directors arrange for Aeneas to be taken ill
    shrouded whispers move over the set

and the shores of Ilium again await her

Aeneas in the Baghdad market

I wake up in the middle of the night

I wake up in the middle of the night
a nagging feeling of something left undone

       sit up in the bed   sheets wrinkled, pooled about the waist
       and about the heart a light panic

vague fears, reasons, unreasons, encroach
impalpable, close as the throat

       what was the thing left undone?

was it the engine left running,
personless, keys in the ignition?

       or was it the numbers, interest
       accruing in stacks?

oh, it is all and none of that
oh, it must be—

       try to lie back down, rigid, on the bed
       beg deep gods for the fade to black

in the mind amounts rise
descend, figures flash

       the bill, that one, unpaid,
       let to mount and grow   also, the tax—

oh, it is all and none of that
oh, it must be—

       I get up, walk to the window where sleeps
       (I think) the neighborhood, uninsomniac

walk to the kitchen, rearrange
bowls, plates in the dish rack

the clock ticks, early minutes click and pass
force myself back onto the bed's iron rack

oh, it is all and none of that
oh, it must be—

I wake up in the middle of the night
a feeling of something left undone—

I must say, my skull aches, you know, from the piles of ash
try to refrain from—cannot help but scratch

soon I succeed, poke a finger down to liquid
green, squish springs of brain—

oh, a tunnel through the planet! I peer through,
at the ready for the next dispatch—

Next Scene: I'm auditioning for the part of a golden-domed haystack
I keep waiting for Millet or the muezzin to call me back.

Scene Three: my life coach is Bill Gates.
holding an infant orphan on his lap

he keeps repeating, Your business plan,
your business plan is off track.

oh, it is all and none of that
oh, it must be—

I wake up in the middle of the night
a fading memory of—

figures on a field arraying and disarraying, and at the base
of the column, in an unknown script—I lean down—

Scene Six: a great sea monster arises from the waters,
myself, handless, below, in the tiniest of rafts

a five-armed man, bulgy-eyed, nears and wheezes
in my ear, Remain. Do not react!

>   just then, the tongue of the sea monster lunges down, lashes
>   me up onto itself. the man calls up to me in air, Just wait. Soon
>   it will retract!

oh, it is all and none of that
oh, it must be—

>   I leave the bed and get a drink of water
>   face pale, hollowed in the mirror—

a clutching feel at the chest

>   on the other side of the mind
>   waking me up at night

figures on a field, arraying and disarraying
myself, readying, for attack and—

>   I leave the bed and get a drink of water
>   face pale, hollowed in the mirror—

in the glass I cannot stare at her
I trip, sit down on the cool of the toilet

>   the light unnightly glaring
>   down upon me

about me I feel it, the early morning's grey cloud
a drifting sorrow, night-still, close as choking

>   I am little red riding hood off to see my grandmother
>   curious, I look inside my basket: there I find the ax

and it is then I remember:
it is only—

in my throat, I find it, that thing
I remember what it was, past waking

chest on knees
leaning forward

I wait   I listen   I sit   I rock
I hear it from within   the sob

and I cry then
for what has been

for what is
for what will be

yes in the quiet of the night I call out
(to whom I do not know)

and I beg—
and I listen to the tiles

to the waking
tiles echo

it is my war

you say to comfort me, But it wasn't you,
it was those others, it wasn't you

     I go to work and after an hour or two
     I empty out my pockets of that sum for it, for Iraq, it is my war

I read the newspaper, tears of the father bereft
Dear sir, I write to him, Forgive me, for it was I who sent your son to war

     there to explode by the side of the road, just before St. Patrick's.
     It was me, I'm to blame, sign it in my name, I did it, it's my war.

I leave my apologies on your doorstep but it is not enough, it is never enough,
it is Iraq, it is my war.

     on the television a girl with hand and face blown off, also a leg
     That's my girl, I think, I made her, look what I made, that's my girl

and I bend over sobbing there
on the couch with the great sorrow of it

     I bought it, I made it
     Iraq, it is my war

Iraq, it is our war
how we grow the poorer

     I buy it, I make it   with the pennies in my pocket
     and even with the nickels, the quarters and—

oh Iraq, it is my war

Aeneas on the public road

one day I am driving through the main thoroughfare
when I happen to see Aeneas out on the street

    sitting by the side of the road
    head bent over

helmet tipped open against the stone wall
she slumps against as cars shush by

    Aeneas has fallen asleep on the public road
    in the helmet a few quarters and one five-dollar bill

I sit beside her here for a while
a semi trembles by, shaking her metal and her tags

    Oh, look! she says, awakens, then laughs
    Someone—has put money in my helmet!

Now, why would they do that? she asks
and to this   I give no answer

and Aeneas stares into her helmet (I)

and Aeneas stares into her helmet

What do you see, I ask Aeneas
When you look in there, what do you see?

     I see—he says   I see nothing you have not seen
     I see what is replete within us

I see the mural with the words scratched in it
I see, held up to the light, the asp

     I see the arguments—sovereign, insolvent
     solvent, unsovereign—

I see the time before the time
before the time of—and also after

     I see the figure striding forth before a dawn
     of a dawn of a dawn of—

(and later, knees to circlet of ribs
alone in shadow crouching)

     I see the figures assembling
     and massing

And you, Aeneas says, turning toward me
I see you amongst them

     And what am I doing, I ask
     moving as if to look

This I cannot tell you, says Aeneas
This—unknown.

     I do, though, think I see it:
     there amongst them, I am setting

upon the ground
something like a branch or a pipe

      dark and wound around with—
      while others, clamoring by me

edge and jostle
rise up between them

      a form of soil, breath
      and shadow   huge, ungainly

and the crowd with their coiled
bodies move it about, hoist it aloft

      Is it good or not, I ask
      pressing my nose almost against it

but the dust of that place
rises up enfolds and

      rising takes   us away
      Oh, I say, as if shaken

falling from it
as it fades

      Aeneas looks then at me
      and I cannot help but notice

the bearing of the warrior
full, upright with—

      his eyes look clearly through me
      minute upon minute

and then he turns his gaze away
brings it once again to rest

          upon the helmet   he strokes it
          slowly then   as if it were   his child

It is difficult to know, he says
Always, it is difficult to know

          and he looks then once
          again into it

flicks a fly
from off its dusted surface.

          against the wall, knees
          drawn up, I ask

What do you see   what
do you see in there?

          Aeneas waits, then says
          I see the beginning of the tree of—

and they descend then into the cedar forest,
sure that they will find and pinion—

          I see that all this—
          and Aeneas wracks his arm about

in wild, whirling movement—
And the high whining of the desert

          sands—and the waters, the rising
          waters, again, and—

and, this earth, bounded by—
and the expanse, the expanse—

          Yes, I say, yes?

The sun and moon as ever
the rosette of destiny

      Which is? I ask—the destiny?
      Oh, that, he says

That has not been made yet.
And about the tomb, he goes on

      at the edges, figures gathered
      in their hands small jars

Oh, it is not a tomb, he says
but a basin   for ablutions

      in their hands small vials
      of the rushing waters, rivulets of—time, or—

and above them, the winged woman
feet, taloned, planted upon the back of the lion

      sun, radiant
      and beside, the lunar sickle

What else, I ask, nearing
Oh, that is all, says Aeneas

      Surely there must be something more, I say
      that you see in there

Aeneas looks again through me
scanning with his eyes my body

      through the skin and through
      even the skeleton

I see everything, says Aeneas
I see everything   that may be

Is it—a kind of clairvoyance? I ask
No, says Aeneas

No. I wouldn't say that.
and he shakes his gaze

        away from me
        zips up his jacket

and sits by it
curled up beside him

        and sits by it
        his helmet

school shooting

we would like to say we did not see
the signs

       we would like to say we were caught
       by surprise

we would like to say this outcome
it was unpreventable

       the bloodshed in particular
       unavoidable

we would like to record
that there was no way

       to save the children of ours
       or the children of others

that there was nothing
we would do differently

       no procedures we
       would alter

in retrospect

       out of respect

for those who have died
for those who have been mutilated

       we cannot truthfully
       claim any of the above

and we will live together with this fate
so long as we live and to the grave

       and indeed   beyond

Aeneas at the Baghdad market

to Baghdad on assignment I am sent
before its start I go sightseeing to the ziggurat

> to the ziggurat of Ur where many a soldier
> climbs the red dirt and looks over the dusted brown plain   there to have
>   his picture taken

back in the streets of Baghdad I am walking
when from amidst the crowd presses toward me a face   so like to that of my Aeneas

> it passes and I turn to look back
> at her clothed all in black

could this be her, could this be my Aeneas?

> doubtful yet I go back to check
> walking against the thrust of the crowd to get back to her

alongside of her now am I
to the side of her walking

> sensing a near presence   she turns slowly her face to look at me
> and from below the shadow of a black scarf are lit the features   of Aeneas

wrapped in a black headscarf
the length of Aeneas now in full hijab

> not knowing what to say, I say, Hello! Are you on leave?
> Oh no! she cries cheerfully. No no, I will not be on leave. I am on full duty now!

And you are—? I ask. Oh, I'm going to market   she motions to the basket over her arm
and the market up ahead   she says, Just beyond that checkpoint

> To do—? I ask. Oh, to do—vegetables, to do—
> Many things, she replies. Right, I say.

Would you come with me? she asks. You can give them your card of identity.
Yes, I say, honored by the invitation, not knowing quite what she means

       *

and so we proceed together, Aeneas and I, arm in arm
she in her black hijab

      and I, I feel myself
      a sort of shield of glory

walking steadily
unsteadily

      toward the checkpoint
      walking   steadily

in the beginning: lines from an ancient
Babylonian tablet

they have come too soon

in a basement in Massachusetts (we call it the cellar), brother and I
he places them, the Mamas and the Papas, on the record player

      in the corner the green humidifier steaming out its gurgled thoughts
      and the wooden table before us, snaking its overpasses and its underpasses

Mama Cass, Mama Cass is in the bathtub
and the stringy-haired skinny guy loves her, doesn't he? doesn't he?

      my brother's hair cut in half a globe, a blonde bowl
      (we are yet not ashamed yet)

Monday, Monday so good to me
You were all I thought you could be

      outside the cellar window frame, white-paned
      the snow upon the ground a white thought covering

But whenever Monday comes it finds me crying
all of the time   Monday, Monday

      oh, how we dance! (actually, we do not dance, we only stand and listen
      as daffodils outside the sill prick heads through glacial soil)

oh the daffodils, they have come too soon
(it was a trick of spring, a trick of lighting)

      soon the daffodils and the pussy willows and the yellow-wine forsythias
        all shall fall
      to the next freeze, the next freeze, sure to be soon

seeing it so, I reach out to his arm, needle-steadying—no, I don't, I just wait
begin to poke at my belly, which appears to have grown in it a hole

      that I have been thinking of entering   yes, I will dig through it
      tunnel to the far reach—a long time in the soil—the East

I've heard you can tunnel through the globe to the other side
which is the same side, in a manner of speaking

    and I think then I do hear something   like an end to something
    disconcerted I hear still a calling   from the far-flung universes

from which I find   my derivation

lines from an ancient Babylonian tablet

When on high the heaven had not been named,
Firm ground below had not been called by name,
Naught but primordial Apsu, their begetter,
And Mummu-Tiamat, she who bore them all,
Their waters commingling as a single body;
No reed hut had been matted, no marsh land had appeared,
When no gods whatever had been brought into being,
Uncalled by name, their destinies undetermined—

     —The Enuma Elish

in the beginning is Tiamat
Thalatte, the sea

  (in the beginning the waters
  were upon the deep)

saltwater sea, Tiamat—
primordial chaos, lifegiving—

  at the edge of the gulf meets
  with Apsu, freshwater sea

and they are mixing their waters
Apsu coupling with Tiamat, Tiamat with Apsu

  from *tehom*, the deep, the abyss
  and from this is birthed all the gods

(the first ones at least)
and so it begins

  o from the primeval waters

  *

and then, one of the newer gods, Enki, of water
and fertile earth, notices that Apsu, disturbed

by the fierce new gods,
has conceived it in his heart to slay them.

and Enki takes it in him
to slay Apsu first

and so Enki slew Apsu.

Kingu, son of Apsu and Tiamat, angered
reports to his mother the slaying.

Tiamat, taking up the battle, pins the tablets of destiny
to the chest of Kingu, and bids him on.

Tiamat fashions with her own hands sea-monsters,
storm kings, scorpion-demons, with these sets Kingu on to fight.

young god Marduk, opposing Tiamat, takes up arms,
determined to win and make himself the new king of the gods.

and with his seven stormwinds Marduk whirls against Tiamat
with his club and spear he sets upon her

and Marduk cleaves Tiamat
cleanly in half

removing the ribs of Tiamat, Marduk uses them to separate heaven
to separate heaven from earth

and the tear channels of Tiamat
become the rivers Euphrates and Tigris

from the son of Tiamat, Marduk removes the tablets of destiny
and indeed crowns himself the king of the gods

＊

again in the streets of Baghdad the prophets see,
in the street, a Kingu make war against a Marduk

    and now Marduk awakens to find the tablets of destiny
    which he had placed in the museum for safekeeping

stolen from his guard
and the museumgoers, in front of empty cases, cry for the absent

    tablets, heritage of—records of
    harvests, heritage taken—

ways, ancient—away
oh, and who shall call them back, the tablets?

    *

    and Inanna, who the people had sent
    on her yearly journey

down into the underworld, kingdom
of her sister, Ereshkigal

    Inanna cannot be found
    and the people look everywhere for her

sure she must be drinking   tea in a little
café if only they   could find her

    sure she must be sweeping
    the streets of   intruders   of all ilk

oh, they look and look
and cannot find her

    *

          it is rumored
          that some obstacle has met

Inanna on her journey
that still she spins

          in the underworld
          deep caverns underground

still Inanna spins
charred corpse

          on the meat hook designated
          by her sister Ereshkigal

and who   who shall
call her back?

          *

          and a child asks, But what of the part of the story
          where she is revived

someone goes down in her place
to replace her

          revive her with a drop
          of sacred water?

those gathered shake their heads
This has not happened, they say.

          and many hands are raised
          I will go! I will go!

Not so easy, the reply.
There is a drought.

Well, we will just go down to the Tigris.
Not so easy, the reply. There is the sewage.

Didn't the Americans fix it?
Oh, but last month the sewage treatment plant was attacked,

They say not to drink it, you'll get typhus.
Surely if we cannot drink it, we cannot give

this water to her,
it might not revive her.

      *

and the moon, it is said, wants them back
the moon yearns for them, the tablets

in which the imprints of her fingernails
were incised

who shall find them, the tablets of destiny?
Tiamat, guardian of knowledge

Tiamat, first sea
once again rising

waters   waters
upon the deep

birds of Iraq

crested lark, trumpeter pigeon
grey wagtail, rook, red-wattled plover

pied kingfisher, European bee-eater
Eurasian collared dove

rock pigeon, spur-winged plover
white-winged tern, black francolins

rufous-backed bush-robin

blackcap, lesser grey shrike
Baghdad Greylag Geese

green sandpiper, barn owl, scops owl
kestrel, moorhen, pied avocet

European roller
bluethroat, white-eared bulbul

yellow wagtail, spotted flycatcher
whinchat, Isabelline wheatear

masked shrike
wryneck, hoopoe

red-backed shrike, magpie, hooded crow
marsh harrier, black-crowned night heron

white-breasted kingfisher
blue-cheeked bee-eater

wryneck, hoopoe

and Aeneas stares into her helmet

and Aeneas stares into her helmet (II)

and Aeneas stretches out her arm before her
in her hand aloft the helmet

     that's a skull that once had tongue in it, she says
     that's a skull that once could sing

Aeneas stares into the upturned helmet
once it knew the future, she says   or thought it knew

     once strode so boldly about the globe
     once it could hear everything thrumming and singing

now it has no ears
still some days it waits for kingdom come

     now it has no eyes
     a mole it crawls, nose upturned, about the earth

now the skull it has no nose
knows not knowing once born in flesh

     now it has no skin   the inside has turned outward, the outside inward
     we are all—it is all toward flaying

now the skull it has no tongue   some one has pulled upon it   'til clean out it has
    come
the tongue it tastes the taste, acrid, of the undiminished sun

     that's the cranium once I envied
     grey axon once joined ranks behind

now pure bones we wait in sky
wait in sky without mind

     ✴

I had a dream in which you and I were buried up to our necks in sand. I came upon us and tried to dig us out with my bare hands, scraping grain after grain, palmfuls of them, away. The more I clawed away, the more of it sifted in, drifted into, caved in about your mouth and into mine, entering, entering, until finally it covered the top of your cranium, the swirl of your crown—sifting, the drifting sand. With a scream in my mouth I awoke, for I knew at that moment you were as good as—

✶

and Aeneas stares into her helmet in the palm outstretched
Aeneas now she sets it down and begins to dig a pit (of her own making)

> she begins to sing, *Oh a pit of clay for to be made*
> *for such a guest is meet*

I ask, But who is the guest? Aeneas replies, Oh the guest!
The guest is all about us! The guest also lodges sore within us

> she replies, The guest is the beloved
> of whom often I have often spoken

Who is the guest? I ask
Now the guest needs speak, says she

> and she drops the helmet
> into the pit of dirt

from her hip, she pulls a branch, and forges it into a shovel
with this she begins to bring deep soil over it

> and Aeneas begins to bury it, the helmet
> to lodge it, the helmet, within deep soil

I reach out
but do not—

> shovelfuls from the land about us
> thrown down upon the helmet

she continues digging and burying frantically and without letup and then, burying
    over—
soon there is nothing but the dabbed-at surface of fresh, upturned soil   fragrant
    with making and enclosing

        helmet pulsing below the surface
        Now, they'll get that, says Aeneas.

staring down and out at the disturbed earth

        Here's a fine revelation, she says
        If only we had the trick to see it

What will you do without your helmet? I ask, Won't you—
Aeneas does not answer but only

        sits down in her fatigues   sand-pebbled
        upon the cut up earth

and by the side of the unmarked grave
head against knees, she begins to shake

        (for it is the grave of many, then, it is the grave of one and many)

tears commingling with dirt
I sit a long time beside her

        until the sun goes down and we are left there at the brink of the earth
        with nothing but the scent of it   soil readied and unreadied   night-sweet

and we sit then a long time with it

deleted scene
Aeneas in Carthage

Aeneas in Carthage

in the early morning the men are quick and eager with the oars
as soil lets go the ship and waves take it, there is a lightening

    ships putting off from shore setting off again into the wide and swelling sea
    to found a great nation, they say, to found a new place in that Latium

and then one of the men cries out,
Look back, look back at that Carthage

    to a man they turn to face that city from which we have come
    faces painted pink-orange with the growing dawn

and it is then I know it before it is known
but even then I do not turn and look

    (it is my great sadness to know it, and so I do not know it)
    —and they watch as a second smoke rises—

and I, cast
back only into the swirl of memory

       ✶

only days ago it seems we were the warriors
who from that flaming city fled (I would like to say we fought bravely)

    fled from Troy into the ships, cast out
    set out upon the seven seas to wander

and that goddess Juno, so set against us (the precise source
of her enmity, I know not)

    Juno on the waters off Troy whips up Aeolus
    to loose wild winds from sea-caves

she seduces Aeolus with promises of sea-nymphs
to stir with the winds the waters

higher than five parapets of Troy
water-cliffs shielding our sight of the horizon

and our ships, thrown up toward clouds
fall back through void to gain sea-bottom

and some of us, feet touching down on sea-sand, open lips
to drink a final water, to find, wide-mawed, the ways of the below

those of us left upon the surface of the waters
sea-sore   spit through storm   cling ever to the prow

through grey sky-sea
a smaller fleet

we wander   rain-ripped, we
drift on

☆

days passing, and then, some sight
in the distance a form

a watery grey
an arc

a nape
of smoke

as we near, it moves into
it gains solidity

there, lilting, a curve of reed
a shore, the men call out, a shore

☆

we trim, we break upon it.
the strongest of us, wobbly-legged, stumbles.

     barnacles grown upon our backs, we follow.

stooped, we vomit seawater upon the sands
some say we are amidst the Phoenicians.

     shaky steps between the reeds.
     oh, to be alive, even weakly.

bearing yet in the brine
the grief of those sea-perished

      ✳

from atop the cliff, men, armed, descend
grasp hold of us. thirsty, we are conducted directly

     to a great hall. in it, a large altar rises to Juno
     she who has so beset us. (and we see how it shall go.)

my men, restrained in the arms of their guards
shrink in their bonds to see it

     I, Aeneas, alone have entered incognito
     by the fog cast by my mother, Venus, made invisible

I wander, I peer at the new friezes, where workmen still tap hammers on stone
   I see there the limbs of the sphinx, there, a lady striding atop them
there, the manes of the double lions

     and there—arms and legs bulging, is that man, tower-built, is not that Hector,
        who fought so valiantly, and yet ate death, as I looked on?
     (and is that—is that not Agamemnon?)

and tears arise in my invisible eyes
to see that even this people, so distant

      have heard of our courage, have scrawled
      in their legends our losses

at the head of the hall, the queen
(for it she who reigns this newly-built palace)

      bids speak one of our men
      who recounts rough treatment

the sovereign to him makes excuses:
in this city, so new, one must beware intruders

      I see we shall have to haste
      quickly away from this place

the queen begins to speak again, now apologizes to our band of men
and bids them full welcome, sorry only that their leader might not speak

      wary, called thus invisibly, I step forward
      from the shield of Venus to be seen in the great hall

from here it happens so strangely
it is a task to say

      *

the queen is Queen Dido, recently widowed (her husband, in the kingdom
of Tyre, killed by her own brother, Pygmalion, man-monster)

      still bearing grief, inexplicably Elissa—as also she is called—
      bids welcome   to the prince Aeneas   and to his men

(could it be only by dint of my mother, Venus?)
risking her own honor, Queen Dido opens to us her hospitality

Queen Elissa welcomes me on walks with her   and the grieving
sovereign and I   indeed take walks together

once, of an afternoon, on a line
between edge of cliff and sea

a storm suddenly lowers in, pelting
us, and we seek

on a downward
path a break

from the wind and we find
a sea-cave   there to refuge   waiting

out the lashing
rains

          *

and Queen Dido offers to the prince Aeneas   the most well-appointed
quarters, adjoining her own   and then, within her own

she bids me obeyed as if I were her consort   partner-ruler
of her Phoenician nation   and soon we are betrothed

she whispers to me, You may call me Elishat
and this, our city, Qart-hadasht

so trusting I cannot fully understand it
yet indeed it widens my heart and it salves my wounds

sating each other in each other, we take, Queen Elissa and I, journeys
aboard a trading vessel   we voyage to Tyre, place of her origin, and then on

to the Babylonians, there to touch tablets
incised of great beauty and newness

guests there, we bend   knees to the altar   of Ishtar
and across the Aegean return to Carthage together

    it is a great thing to rest in Carthage, at the breast of the Phoenicians
    as I lie upon her silken sheets, and feel the breeze from off the slow, the Punic sea

I mark the distance from the briny reaches
to which we so long had been exiled

    strange that after such a journey   I should recline   as on the rocking
    of another sea   beside this doe-eyed Dido

      in her finding my partner

    *

some days I lie across her midriff and query her on the ire of Juno
Explain me that, I ask   she replies that it began in the judgment of Paris

    who, choosing amongst three goddesses the most beautiful, passed over Juno
    slighted, she now projects into a near future

when you—Dido touches me upon the chest—will found a great people in a Rome,
and your descendants will make war upon her—our—Carthage

    But this I will not do! I say   I ask, Can you not assure her?
    Can I? asks Dido. Can I assure Juno you shall never set off from this shore

to man your battleships to put up on some other shore, there against the natives
to wage war, clearing through violence the land

    and naming it your Rome? surprised, I say, Is that the plan? Dido tsks.
    Don't you read your own materials? she points. there by the bedside—

I had not noticed it—a pile of bulletins, stamped with the imprimatur of Zeus.
Haven't you noticed these? she asks. Not really, I reply. they must have been
    dropped

126

off by Mercury. they all say the same thing, with increasing degrees of urgency
as one moves to the top of the pile. among the most recent: Fabled Prince
Aeneas

Declines His Fate. Waylaid in Carthage. Let's Get Him Back on Track. Maven
Dido Distracts Prince From Destiny. An Empire Waits to be Born. Only Aeneas

Can Do It. Remind Him of His Fate. What is this pulp? I ask. Dido looks
at me, clear-eyed. These are the commands of your gods and people.
According to this, I'm

the distraction, she says. You're not—my fate is here with you. I have
no other fate, I say. That's not what they think, she says. that night, I go

to sleep, tormented. in the middle of a moon ray arrives Mercury,
feet-wings thrushing like a hummingbird's. he is not indirect:

detained here in Carthage, I desecrate the memory of my father's shade.
I deny this. What greater reply to grief than to birth a new love? I ask. Quit the
mealy-

mouthed mewling, says Mercury. You've got a destiny to fulfill. It is a
question
of honor. I reply, What greater honor to love where one finds oneself loved?

Elissa is not a lover, he says. She is—a local girl, a temptress.
A local girl who has shown me something, I say. Might not that

be greater than any preordained destiny? Might not the empire of love
be the fullest we might know? I find myself astonished here in Carthage,

I plead. Could one ask for a greater gift? Might not this be destiny,
to be changed in a love unexpectedly given?

Not—how—dominions—are—made, says Mercury. Maybe you're wrong
in that, I say. Maybe that's exactly how true dominions are made.

and I can feel my heart pulsing as I speak, our hearts pulsing through the sea.
No, says Mercury. Remember duty, remember filial piety. This is what

    your father would have wanted, this justice. Are you sure? I ask.
    Take these, he says; he shoves some bulletins at me, points at figures,

graphs. We have it on the surest intelligence, he says. Your command is clear.
Do not betray your father, he says. Have I ever—I protest.

    Don't begin now, says Mercury. Don't betray him—for anything,
    he says, and, before departing, looks sidelong at the bed, where lies my
       sleeping lover.

and I spend a long time there with the figures, trying to sort
them out, truth from vision, vision from proffered truth,

    betrayal from faith, enlargement from contentment, nation from self,
    love from love. in the labyrinth of moonlight I founder

upon the shoals of knowing. and there—it is a hazard and still now hounds
me to recall—in the ray of moonlight I put on my sandals, and a shirt, and I walk
    out of that room

    down to the crew's quarters; there, I wake the men. and as if they had been
      waiting only
    for that signal, with all alacrity they leap to, readying the ships.

    *

without one word, then, I left her.
as the dawn flushed the waters.

    I am ashamed to speak it. we rowed toward that future.
    I thought it important.

and as we did, we all smelled it in the air
something burning, something amiss—

and I felt then, of a sudden, we should
turn back, quickly—but it seemed too late—

wasn't it already too late? should I not have stayed
there with my betrothed, my lover,

    to whom I had entrusted my self?
    I left that trust for another

I felt I owed. we smelled
the scent of it, then.

    the men with their faces turned back toward shore
    and by now you, you know what it is.

you know what it would take me
a journey down to the river Styx finally to know:

    that smoke was the rising body
    of my lover, Dido, who in her grief

had thrown herself on her own
funeral pyre. that second smoke,

    her own.
    and now, mine.

        with her I left a part
        of what I might have been

            there
            in Carthage.

of excuses,
I make none.

    away from her burning body—I'll pretend
    I didn't know it was hers—away I turned

and looked full face
toward that Rome.

       *

my men even then whittling their weapons
for the next battle

      against the people who did not yet know
      fields, courtyards would be cleared

for our future
city.

       *

and in my dreams I am often there, still in Carthage
even so in between the thighs of my Dido

      taking boat rides to the Babylonians
      touching the tablets, records of harvests

and all that is gone
is not yet gone yet

      oh Dido, would I had died
      in your arms—would I

had died not without
but within you

notes

The epigraph is an excerpt from Walt Whitman's poem "Turn, O Libertad."

p. 51: "ample upon the painted sands" makes use of the term "orthodox innovator," coined by Stephen Skowronek, professor of social and political science at Yale University.

p. 57: "Interrogation #2356" draws upon my reading of *Inside the Wire: A Military Intelligence Soldier's Eyewitness Account of Life at Guantanamo* (Penguin, 2005) by Erik Saar with Viveca Novak.

p. 89: "I wake up in the middle of the night" includes the image of touching one's brain, inspired by an anecdote related by Atul Gawande in his article "The Itch" in the June 30, 2008 issue of *The New Yorker*.

p. 105: "they have come too soon" includes italicized lyrics from "Monday, Monday," written by John and Michelle Phillips, recorded by The Mamas and the Papas (Dunhill Records, 1966). Where I have written "You were all I thought you could be," the original line is "It was all I hoped it would be."

p. 107: The epigraph for "lines from an ancient Babylonian tablet" is an excerpt from the beginning of the *Enuma Elish*, or the Babylonian Creation Epic, from *Alpha: the Myths of Creation*, by Charles H. Long, p. 80–91, translated by Alexander Heidel, in *The Babylonian Genesis* (University of Chicago Press, 1942). Another useful translation of this epic has been made by N. K. Sandars in *The Poems of Heaven and Hell from Ancient Mesopotamia* (Penguin Classics, 1971). In composing my poem, I also drew upon Wikipedia's July 2008 entry for "Tiamat."

p. 112: Except for the blackcap, the birds mentioned in "birds of Iraq" can be found, with accompanying photos, at www.lauraerickson.com/bird/Places/Iraq/IraqBirdsGallery.html.

p. 115: In "and Aeneas stares into her helmet (II)," the italicized lines are from *Hamlet*, Act 5, Scene 1, and the second couplet alters Shakespeare's "That skull had a tongue in it, and could sing once." The link to Hamlet's signature gesture was suggested to me by Antonio Piccolboni. The dour Dane actually says, "Here's fine revolution an we had the trick to see 't."

acknowledgements

"where is the war?" and "discourse on impossibility" appeared, in previous versions, in the Fall 2005 issue of *nocturnes*.

I would like to thank the many people who generously offered their creative powers toward this project. Thanks to Andrea Selch of Carolina Wren Press for her stalwart guidance, and to Kay Robin Alexander for her proofing, and to Lesley Landis for her design. Thanks to Carolina Wren Press board member Patrick Herron for his sustaining encouragement during the revision process. Thanks to Ben Steinberg and Ruth Schenk for reading many versions and patiently offering precise advice. Thanks to Pablo Ortega López for listening to my concept for the book and bringing it to life in the cover artwork more fully than I could have hoped for. Thanks to Alison Martin and Judy Tuwaletstiwa for early discussions about cover images. Thanks to Carol Ciavonne, Polly Chatfield, Jane Mead, and Evelyn Averbuck (1912-2007) for having read early versions of the manuscript. Thanks to Stephanie Ivanoff for her enthusiastic notes, and to Liza Featherstone, Kate Horsley, and Rachel Shuh for their answers to specific questions; for the photo, thanks to Andrea Ferreira. Thanks to those who read the almost-finished manuscript: Mary Graham, Alison Martin, and my mother, Leslie Kain. Thanks to my father, George A. Higgins, for his continuing love and encouragement. And I thank the many acquaintances and friends who heard about the project and extended their support, for in doing so, they nourished its vision; I offer to you my deep gratitude.

The text of the book is typeset in 10-point Minion.
The book was designed by Lesley Landis Designs
and printed by Patterson Printing.